Berryman's Fate:

A Centenary Celebration in Verse

BERRYMAN'S FATE:

A Centenary Celebration in Verse

Philip Coleman
Editor

ARLEN
HOUSE

Berryman's Fate: A Centenary Celebration in Verse

is published in 2014 by
ARLEN HOUSE
42 Grange Abbey Road
Baldoyle
Dublin 13
Ireland
Phone/Fax: 353 86 8207617
Email: arlenhouse@gmail.com
arlenhouse.blogspot.com

Distributed internationally by
SYRACUSE UNIVERSITY PRESS
621 Skytop Road, Suite 110
Syracuse, NY 13244–5290
Phone: 315–443–5534/Fax: 315–443–5545
Email: supress@syr.edu

978–1–85132–112–4, paperback

Typesetting by Arlen House

Printed lithographically in Dublin

Front cover photograph, taken by John Berryman on a visit to Dublin in 1937, and back cover manuscript lines from Dream Song 312, are reproduced courtesy of Kate Donahue and the Estate of John Berryman (c) 2014

Contents

Philip Coleman

INTRODUCTION

In one of the 'Apparition' poems in his collection *Theories and Apparitions* (2008), Mark Doty has a vision of John Berryman, sitting in 'the window / of the Eros Diner'. It is an oblique nod, surely, to Dream Song 4, but in Doty's poem Berryman is decidedly uninterested in the surrounding diners. We find him

eating alone,
back against the wall,
face tilted down toward
his meal, iconic thick glasses

glinting like the sidewalk
in the cold, iconic thick beard
nodding a little as he lifts
his spoon (13)

Doty's repeated use of the word 'iconic' in reference to Berryman's 'thick glasses' and 'thick beard' reinforces a popular visual image of the poet. However, Doty's poem also speaks to the misguided critical assumption that Berryman was a poet who failed to engage with the world around him. In Doty's 'Apparition' the speaker laments the fact that Berryman is 'so happy / that a plate's in front / of him he never bothers / to look up at me.' The idea, on one level, is that Berryman was so concerned with himself that he couldn't be bothered to consider anyone else, but this view is bound up with the 'iconic' image of the bearded bard that is challenged when one considers the actual contours of the poet's career. Certainly when it came to engaging with other poets and artists – including musicians and painters, from Brian Boydell to Ben Shahn – the story of

Berryman's positive engagements with others complicates the image of withdrawal that is suggested in Doty's poem.

There is a lot more to Doty's 'Apparition': it is also a brilliant evocation of the poet in his private element if not in self-imposed isolation. No matter how one reads it – whether as an affirmation of a particular image of the poet or as an invitation to reconsider the old 'icon' – 'Apparition' suggests that Berryman persists in the contemporary poetic imagination in ways that continue to inspire, provoke, unsettle and delight many writers. In his own lifetime, and in the decade immediately following his tragic death in 1972, he grew to have many admirers. As Michael Hofmann has argued, however, things appeared to go 'rather quiet around Berryman' (viii) – at least in critical terms – during the 1980s and after. This may have been the case in criticism, but Berryman's importance to many of the poets who came after him has never been in doubt. The publication of a new volume of selected poems edited by Daniel Swift, together with re-issues of three of his book-length works with introductions by major poets (April Bernard, Henri Cole, and Michael Hofmann) in 2014 is a testament to Berryman's persistent appeal to contemporary readers in his centenary year. This book – *Berryman's Fate: A Centenary Celebration in Verse* – celebrates Berryman from another perspective by gathering together poems written by over fifty poets from a wide range of cultural contexts. The poems gathered here have either been written specifically for this volume or they were composed previously with Berryman in mind. In one way or another, they all affirm the importance of Berryman's example in early twenty-first century poetic culture on both sides of the Atlantic.

This is not the first time a book of this kind has been published. In 1976, for example, Marguerite Harris edited a volume with the wonderful title *A Tumult for John Berryman*, published in San Francisco by Dryad Press, which included contributions from Michael Berryhill, Donald Davie, David

Ignatow, Ted Kooser, Robert Lowell, William Matthews, Judith Minty, and others. The word 'tumult' seems right for Berryman in some respects: his own work is often characterised by the experience of agitation, disturbance, and violent emotion. 'Henry sounds like eighty Viet Congs', as Berryman puts it in Dream Song 333, but in the same Song he writes that 'Henry's listeners / make up a gallant few.' (265) *A Tumult for John Berryman* celebrated the fact that more than a few readers of the poet's work attended to it with creative intent. By the same token, *Berryman's Fate: A Centenary Celebration in Verse* shows that the poet and his work mean as much to readers today – and especially to readers who are also writers – as it did in the decade immediately following his death. *Berryman's Fate,* then, is a birthday gift to Berryman's shade and a reflection of his living presence in the creative lives of the poets who have written for this volume. In a posthumously published Dream Song entitled 'Henry's Fate', written in 1968, he wrote: 'All projects failed, in the August afternoon / he lay & cursed himself & cursed his lot' (*Henry's Fate* 32). Berryman may have doubted the success of his work and its value for his own and later generations: 'In official rime / the official verdict was: dead', 'Henry's Fate' concludes. *Berryman's Fate* refutes that 'verdict'. In the various forms of 'rime' included here Berryman and his work live in the most profound and unexpected ways, affecting both the formal and thematic decisions taken by poets working within often radically different traditions, from Ireland and the United Kingdom to South Africa and the United States.

In an essay based on a talk given at the University of Minnesota in 1973, the self-proclaimed 'Anglo-Sotan' poet Michael Dennis Browne wrote: 'I don't know whether John Berryman would have been pleased to know of the extent to which his own work affected my own at an important time in my writing life, but I like to imagine that he would' (9). Berryman himself was never particularly shy about letting his 'heroes' (as he calls them in one of the poems from *Love & Fame*) know how much he admired them. From his early discipleship of W.B. Yeats to his passionate advocacy of certain friends who were also poets – most notably Dylan Thomas and Delmore Schwartz – Berryman was a great *constructive* critic, often going to great pains to explain why he believed certain aspects of a work were more successful than others. This is certainly true of his engagement with Schwartz. At the same time, Berryman was always willing to acknowledge how much he had himself borrowed from those he admired and, indeed, in an interview first published in the *Harvard Advocate* in 1969 he readily admitted that the basic formal template for *The Dream Songs* was taken from Yeats:

> Yes, well, the stanza is complicated. It goes 5-5-3-5-5-3, 5-5-3-5-5-3, 5-5-3-5-5-3 – that's the business – and it's variously rhymed, and often it has no rhyme at all, but it sounds as if rhymed. That I got from Yeats – three six-line stanzas. His songs don't really resemble mine, but I did get that from him. It's rather like an extended, three-part sonnet.

In the first part of this book over thirty contemporary poets have written what many of them have termed 'Dream Songs', but the extent to which they attempt to imitate, borrow from, or repudiate Berryman's example is as difficult to define as it is to say precisely how much the American poet 'got from Yeats', apart from the example of the 'three six-line stanzas' used in *The Dream Songs*. As he puts it in Dream Song 312, in which he confronts the 'majestic Shade' of Yeats:

> did I read your lesson right? did I see through
> your phases to the real? your heaven, your hell
> did I enquire properly into? (244)

There was much more to Berryman's engagement with Yeats than the imitation of a formal example, in other words, and the same is true of the poems gathered here which appear, on the surface, to mimic the Dream Song form.

Some of the poems included in the first part of the book are from longer sequences or series of poems, while others are stand-alone lyrics. All of them engage in different ways with both the formal and thematic preoccupations of Berryman's work. There are poems here that play with the three six-line stanza form that Berryman made his own but borrowed, by his own admission, from Yeats. There are also pieces, however, in which this formal arrangement is re-thought and disrupted, where lines are added or left out, syntax and language are re-worked in ways that seem to owe nothing at all to Berryman's own unique example. Some of the poems gathered here refer to the persona of Henry, the presiding character of *The Dream Songs*, but in others Henry is replaced by other figures, some of whom appear here in print for the first time. Familiar Dream Songs, such as Dream Song 29, are recast here in stunningly new and frankly unexpected ways, but Berryman also emerges in the second part of the book as a poet whose lessons in the crafting of elegy, for example, and in the construction of self, are shown to be of great importance to a diverse group of contemporary poets. There are poems here that celebrate the imagination and the world of dreams, but there are also poems of both the body and the body politic, of love and loss, longing and belonging, travel and home. There are Dream Songs of different kinds – there are even some poems that might be described as *half* Dream Songs – but all of the poems are offered in celebration of Berryman's lasting achievement and in celebration of his centenary year.

This book therefore offers a sampling of writing by contemporary poets for whom what Michael Dennis Browne calls Berryman's distinctive 'atmosphere of mind' represents undeniable if not irresistible creative and imaginative power. There are many other examples that could have been included here, in addition to those gathered in *A Tumult for John Berryman* in 1976. The initial inspiration for this project was the inclusion of a 'Dream

Song' in the title-sequence of Dennis O'Driscoll's last collection of poems before his untimely death in 2012, *Dear Life*. In this poem O'Driscoll refers to and quotes from Berryman's poem 'Henry's Understanding', which was published in *Delusions, etc.* (1972) (O'Driscoll 102). Another Irish poet, Dermot Healy, has a poem called 'Recovery' in his collection *The Ballyconnell Colours* (1992), which also refers to Berryman's late work, while British poet Simon Barraclough's 'The Dream Song of Saddam Hussein', from *Los Alamos Mon Amour* (2008) is a highly politicised re-writing of Dream Song 1. Tyehimba Jess's long poem 'Mirror of Slavery / Mirror of Chicanery: The Freed Songs of Berryman / Brown' – 'in which the escaped slave and traveling mesmerist Mr. Henry 'Box' Brown blackens the voice of the poet Mr. John Berryman's 'Henry' from Dream Songs and liberates him(self) from literary bondage!' (78) – is another remarkable recent re-working, with particular emphasis on Berryman's treatment of race. The complex sonic echo chamber of Berryman's poetry is also a source for Brittany Cavallaro and Rebecca Hazelton's *No Girls No Telephones* (2014), a work in which 'Brittany had the idea of writing an opposite of a John Berryman Dream Song, and suggested that Rebecca write an opposite of that opposite' (28). In addition to these explicit formal and thematic engagements with Berryman's work by contemporary poets, a case might be made for including work by a poet like David Harsent, whose poetry has been likened to Berryman's by Sean O'Brien. The title of Harsent's collection *Fire Songs* (2014) sounds a clear Berrymanian note, but in addition to his attraction to the longer sequence and a certain baroqueness of diction, a poem like 'Fire: *a song for mistress Askew*' also engages in creative conversation with Berryman's *Homage to Mistress Bradstreet* in ways that seem more than coincidental.

Berryman's Fate: A Centenary Celebration in Verse is not intended to be a manifesto declaring the American poet's influence on contemporary poetry, but the poems gathered here speak for themselves and for the interests and inclinations of those who wrote them. Beyond these poems there are many bodies of work that differ and diverge from Berryman's example in ways that cannot be contained by critical labels and definitions, no more than the poet's own work should be defined in relation to a single school or categorisation. *Berryman's Fate,* finally, like Berryman's work in itself, affirms and celebrates the art of poetry as 'one of the most important tools we have for understanding human reality', as the poet put it in an interview conducted in Dublin for the BBC in 1967. As he wrote in Dream Song 370, written in the same year:

> When he dressed up & up, his costumes varied
> with the southeast wind, but he remained aware.
> Awareness was most of what he had.

This book celebrates and responds to Berryman's 'varied' costumes and voices, but it also reflects the extent to which contemporary poets continue to be aware of his incomparable gift and genius.

Works Cited

John Berryman, *His Toy, His Dream, His Rest* (New York: Farrar, Straus and Giroux, 1968).

__. *Henry's Fate and Other Poems,* ed. John Haffenden (New York: Farrar, Straus and Giroux, 1977).

—. *Poems Selected by Michael Hofmann* (London: Faber and Faber, 2004).

Michael Dennis Browne, 'Henry Fermenting: Debts to the Dream Songs', in *What the Poem Wants: Prose on Poetry* (Pittsburgh: Carnegie Mellon Press, 2009): 9–24.

Brittany Cavallaro and Rebecca Hazelton, *No Girls No Telephones* (Black Lawrence Press, 2014).

Mark Doty, *Theories and Apparitions* (London: Jonathan Cape, 2008).

David Harsent, *Fire Songs* (London: Faber and Faber, 2014).

Tyehimba Jess, 'Mirror of Slavery / Mirror of Chicanery: The Freed Songs of Berryman / Brown'. *Jubilat* 24 (2013): 78–94.

Dennis O'Driscoll, *Dear Life* (London: Anvil Press Poetry, 2012).

ACKNOWLEDGEMENTS

The editor and publisher wish to thank the following for granting permission for work, which has appeared previously in print elsewhere, to be included in this book:

Harry Clifton for 'Wrecker's Lantern' (from *Throat Songs*), which was published in Philip Coleman and Philip McGowan, eds. *'After thirty Falls': New Essays on John Berryman* (Rodopi, 2007).

Martin Dyar and the editors of the *New Hibernia Review*, for 'Margaret', published in *New Hibernia Review* (Summer 2014).

John Matthias and Shearsman Books for 'While Reviewing John Berryman's *The Freedom of the Poet*', first published as part of an essay on Berryman's work in *Who Was Cousin Alice? and Other Questions* (Shearsman, 2011).

Hugh Maxton and Duras Press for '*Tote Stadt*', first published in *Same Bridge Perhaps and other fugitive poems* (Duras, 2013).

Gerry Murphy and the Dedalus Press for 'You Did and You Did', first published in *Extracts From The Lost Log-Book of Christopher Columbus* (Dedalus, 1999).

Thanks to Raiana Grieme, Kathryn Hujda, Cecily Marcus, and Jennifer Torkelson of the University of Minnesota Libraries for their help in preparing digital copies of manuscript and photographic materials used on the cover of this book. The front cover photograph was taken by John Berryman on a visit to Dublin in 1937, while the back cover reproduces the first stanza of Dream Song 312 from a manuscript fair copy. For granting permission to use those materials very special thanks are due to Kate Donahue and the Estate of John Berryman.

The editor wishes to thank the following people in particular for their help with this project: John F. Deane, Theo Dorgan, Martin Dyar, Alan Hayes, Kathryn Maris, Niamh NicGhabhann and Gerard Smyth. Many thanks also to the poets who gave so generously of their time and energy to contribute to this book.

This book is dedicated, by the editor, to the memory of Dennis O'Driscoll (1954–2012).

PART I

Simon Barraclough

ALIEN DREAM SONG

There burst out, once, a thing from Kane's heart
só ugly, if he had a hundred years
& more, & weeping, sleepless, in all them time
Kane could not make good.
Starts again always in Kane's throat
the little cough somewhere, a ripping, a tear.

And there is another thing he has in mind
like a grave alien face a thousand years
would fail to blur the still profiled reproach of. Ghastly,
with sliding jaws, he attends, blind.
All the beacons say: too late. This is not for tears;
thinking.

But never did Kane, as he thought he did,
end anyone, cocoons her body up
and hide the pieces, where they may be found.
He knows: he went over the ship, & nobody's missing.
Often he reckons, in the cryo-tube, them up.
Nobody is ever missing.

Ciaran Berry

Postcard from Connecticut

From this in-between state where, out of hate
for sports, you learned to sing,
I send greetings, John Allyn Berryman,
gone off downstream. I hit
a long high note out on this xylophone –
your instrument, I think.

Orpheus to our constant orphanage,
stand-up comic, offbeat,
today, I smoke one of your cigarettes,
try out your favourite gags,
your false moustache, the high heels and lorgnettes.
I wonder what Henry

would make of this, and if it's him I spy
next door with that lawnmower.
Of leaf blowers and snow tyres, we dream these days
in this after dawn light,
in which I chicken scratch this note to say,
again, wish you were here.

Steven Bliss

A LATE SONG

For John Berryman

Forty years gone, I mourn forgotten Henry,
who leapt to a foreknown end & moulders safe
with father & rival Cal –
both whom he not forgave – where drink
& drugs no longer derange. Rest
in sort of peace now, pal.

Success wreckt him – oh, & alcohol.
Unwrit his Shakespeare, untoucht those Folger Folios,
him fixt in some dingy bar.
Tired to pursue new women, clinging to Kate,
he versed more easy, human like, content
to re-rub old scars.

Parcht a year or more, he half-found God –
Lost – a lurch, down from the wintry bridge
to miss somehow the river
& splatter shoreline cinders, blank
cheque in his pocket, poems still in the press;
his horribles over.

Michael Dennis Browne

FROM *HIS ANXIETY*

It's complicated how his sleep and him
Fell out, who were not ever, to begin with,
Close. Some bitterness? You betcha. There are words
A paying crowd would not be disappointed
At. But sedge his eyes, and no birds sing.
Once he smelled smoke, but blaze there never were.

His pals are in the trenches as we speak,
Dodging the gas, the loony cannisters,
Dodging the worms, swerving to stay on track.
The chums insist their march around his room.
His pals have scarpered and will not be back.
Their bones belong in wind. So long all that.

Him silence drifting not from down the sky.
No one will sign for anything. *Aucun signature.*
He'll have to pay you at the river rate;
You might just have to drown, his trust to earn.
O bland inversions, how their beauties faded
To where they kneel for mercy in the snow.

Siobhan Campbell

Ravens

Ravens in their *ruaile buaile* hear the tick of season-tuning
trees
they colonise like something moral to be despised.
Out of the regions of the tourist dark they surprise by being
here, by being real. I am aware that our language crosses
swords.
Your capped heads, your jagged faces, not all one colour, no,
you are blue and grey gradations, you are indigo inked to
the red
edge. The stones you drop crack open a rival's eggs.

There is a smite of forever in the calluses behind your beak
though some of you ail and moult and cheep rather than
caw.
You are not omens of something happening elsewhere,
petty deaths
on the other side of the hill nor votes casting a future of
transaction,
a tit for tat, a blind eye bought for less than it cost last year.
Lone selves, nothing as trite as foretelling in your
congregation.

How to approach you, how to be in the same acre? How not
to ask
why you screech now, wheeling over the trees, or why you
quieten,
each staking yourselves out. You do this. You show
aspiration up
and dress it down. Are you most apt for how little is
known?
This is not wild. This is not idle. Ravens have said it all,
almost.
Here comes the horseman, may I say 'pass by'?

Walter Cannon

Birth

William could never get his history right,
his story-wright culled out
the shadows of his birth now 69 years
ago, but gone the memory, flown
with mother and father and country, the nets
patterned him down

a rabbit hole constricted, squirmed his
comfort dark soft & breath-
less, grasping crawling moaning
forward, push & push, O smaller,
gasp in the dark corridor tightening
membraned endless slime his

pant for life. Some good he means
to do, O, O, O, smaller by
tunnel twisted suffocation knot
onely breath breathe ga
sp   end   dark visible
ness   cry!

Jonathan Creasy

DAKOTA DREAM (UNSUNG)

Sound, sense – imploring; that those who go here
go where wind once shook our cities.
Laughter, learning, distinction:
distraction for the bored and deadly boring.
Writing books, a doubled edge –
No use (she knew) to take the pledge.

But I who walk here, and friends beside,
hidden go among them.
Tried, time-tested – timorous behind the eyes.
You (as the glow-worm lighted as it dies)
find truth in talk,
believe credentialed lies.

Welter in civilized life,
the voices of children removed & undone.
Grace sure takes its liberties with the young.
Water to wash you, wake you with sound in soft pitch –
Keep this music close to heart & to hand;
sing the Lake & River below the Bridge.

Dublin, 9 July 2014 (one year gone)

Tony Curtis

HENRY IN THE MIRROR

Darkened his hair, his tears disappeared,
inapprehensible he gave up books
nourished instead by nature,
his soul fed on clouds & hills
something quietly happened to Henry, he turned
off, no, turned down the burner inside himself,

smaller & bluer the answers stood
his for the taking, his to remember,
these Henry found almost too much
implying light cures for the dark cave of grief,
Walt's 'tall oak' a symbol he could
Incorporate slowly into his life,

into his night he began returning to books.
Embarrassed Henry began with Yeats
and the older Delmore Schwartz,
of which the pain was far too great
these poems of Delmore's weighed on his eyes,
whilst Henry's beard grew grey & dusty.

Gerald Dawe

Via Dolorosa

'Nobody in the world knows where I am' (Dream Song 355)

Groggy with the height
and wind in his ears
and, for all we know,
the sound of the mother
going on at him,
poor Mr Bones decided

he was off, a lurid flight,
a shocker of a journey,
away from those who loved
and in return were loved,
with no rhyme or reason why
but for the busted-up bits

and pieces of the past,
Mr Bones, all heart, cried
his goodbye and was spotted
only once, a ghost already,
in the resistless fall down
to the river's demented dark.

John F. Deane

Reynolds, staunch Sagittarian,
aimed always high, both barrels of his shotgun
screwed to the dark shape
in the topmost branches of the dawdling sycamore;
and he, Mister H, was truthful when he said
that he was steeped, steeped, steeped

in luck, though I'd say graced
with sequoia-growth of talent. One shoe
dangling
bright Reynolds to a halt:

yet it is again dark-green wreathe-time
in our world, threaded holly branches with their blood-
  berries,
pine-cones,
that nature's baby Reynolds knitted fast
with his knuckled fingers and thumbs
out of an overburdening love.

Peter Denman

An Elegy for S.H., the lovely man

No, not at Henry's bidding. We went and found
in the tidy town of Garvagh the wooded mound
topped with its little pyramid.
The marker marked a tomb built long ago
but never used as such – Mr Bones: is that so? –
Well, no bones therein hid.

And keeping south, (take out out and see)
we stopped in Diddy's for cake and tea
alongside the street
where lorries carried on in rushing past
and buses too (south first & last).
Initials meet.

Then came we lastly to the bend in the road
and pulled in just as Mr Bones had showed
– had showed de how and where.
Ah, we'd never step into his grave as quick
cornered as he is, under that crossed stick.
And so there so there so there.

Maurice Devitt

FROM *DUBLIN DREAM SONGS*

You said the case was open and shut
– brown leather. Returned to your lobster,
pink and distracted.
Jammett's at 4pm – or was it Paradiso at 2? –
half the staff leaving
the other half not.

Rising late you had poured yourself into
the day: mismatched shoes, a shadow
and that scarlet tie,
the one you said you hated, or was it
that it hated you – ever since it saw you
in the mirror ?

Even though you were sleeveless, you had a way
of wearing your heart – not showy just close
enough to hide despair.
You smoked – you never smoked – & spoke
of Delville, not 2-up, 2-down, but a house
is still a house.

Isobel Dixon

Dream Song for John Berryman

She sets her wineglass delicately down
and Henry harrumphs inwardly
at all the world's geometry and fission nuclear
in thát. Then smitten, smarting
from her wide indifference, he spills
his own. Hubbub and salted tables

and the stain admonishes all night. A map,
lost territory. Will they, reproachful hosts,
invite him back, or shoulder coldly to the C-list?
Calmati, Henry!
O, Mr Bones I knows the score.
Henry must tame the lust-quest –

knees, whiskey phantasies, the conscience
unappeasable. Wreckt, wracked, there hover
over Henry hummingbirds, flown in
from gentler climes. Henry slo-mos their wings,
the flexing tints. And sips. But can Henry write it?
Reader, he díd, and was desired.

Timothy Donnelly

CLARITIN-D

What illness in my limbs others'
rodomontade instills with tin
trumpets doesn't pass the way it did
when under rhododendron
past purple the early I rose from an hour
outstretched on ancient dirts

to forgive what there was to. A leaf
dome above me, above that
another, then the washed-out sky
with nonpersons in it put there
to take note of ... It's only ever persons
that talk to me now, and how

they've worsened I can't say except
dramatically. Myself, I take it
I've matured into a bluster of
some size, as what isn't here has blown
off to Pawtucket, & every leaf
that turns is turned away from me.

Tyler Flynn Dorholt

From *AWAY*

The filmmaker presents to be a reacher,
a lean operation about how the whole mirror
is a room inching toward people's houses,
how away can romanticize & shoulder
what is to be done for infrastructure,
the body to construct lyrics or blouses & spheres

down over the flap, throat afloat in the loft with
our hands hawking the middle nothing into endless
options, but we often have more options than we think
in the failing process, innocence contained in a half-circle,
to be unusual or experienced before standing inside love,
so many photographs at night, angels fooled by pain,

even in the elm these works on video, yet you are so
rushed around in gestures flesh protects, in the world of
preferring the careful posture, that the paradigm of order
holds in, starting up titanic a dream where you come across
concept to flower a pot of the proper, where water
rushes in to crumble the windows.

Martin Dyar

MARGARET

I am often asked about the success of the group.
And to go around invoking heaven wouldn't do.
I tell them baldly that our system of healing

is above all others. When an interviewer laughs,
my tongue tends to barrel: a layman's giftedness
spliced to cool seniority, a jauntiness of diction

for the intangibles. Margaret has been a handy case.
Psychiatric through her thirties, she came to us.
Our deeming her a spirit biochemically fettered

was a breakthrough. Large doses of music therapy
clipped her blackness and slowed her to a fuller life:
hillwalking, Jack Russell pups, some admin

at our offices. There's a book about her journey
gone to press. But one could never tell Margaret's
story completely. You see, it could not be accepted

that the drumming left us all almost deranged,
or that a river appeared in the conference centre floor
from which a muscular Christ bore up the cure.

Zack Finch

DREAM ORDEAL

'Jesus Christ,' admit it,
'Is the one true literary critic.'
Problem is, I never
Venerated myself a proper Christian.
So I guess, this minute,
I'm damned to be damned.

Knock on wood, like it's a priest's booth
Or an eyetooth, standing out
Loose in the natural light
Like a wobbly chorister.
What I want, I want outright:
To be confused, by God,

For the lamb boy, Isaac,
Propped under an imaginary sky,
Ribbed with clouds, a worsted blue
Dream of psychic shudder,
Breathing air that doesn't matter
Above the firewood skillfully arranged.

Leontia Flynn

DREAM SONG FOR LAWRENCE

In Edinburgh in 1999
occasionally flies but chiefly snot and gum
were your twin dark terrors
(You showed me these so I would show you mine);
Your OCD was *not* mere 'clean freak-dom'.
You scrubbed, took showers –

for which I blamed your long-lost Commodore dad –
the 4 minute nuclear warning was so much blether,
he'd said as a kid
'We'll die right here!'. But Your Irish grandmother,
I liked. She'd burned her arm off in the fire.
You drank like she did.

And I like you and like folk in a fable we fled
to that third floor, soon-to-scrubbed and defended flat.
You give me the present
– of not, like, talking to people or thinking ahead.
Cracking a bottle, you grinned once 'life's too short!',
though, with you, it wasn't.

Mark Granier

Berryman In Ryan's, 1967

No wonder. Here's a hunched
serious man being serious
as a leap in the dark, for sure.
So much so
it's almost caricature. Eyes
blaze and slumber,

framed in black specs heavy
as a library, and that great
Father Time beard poring
over and into – what? Well, I guess
it may as well be us
boring. I don't see

anyone else here besides
those who are always missing. I don't know
what dreams in there: a drift
of empty beds, horizons hard
as winter, something low and far
too high for any stumbler.

Iggy McGovern

Just walk on by
Only fools rush in
How many roads must a man
No one could take your place
Bring back that loving feeling
Ebony and ivory

Ride on, see you
Regina coeli laetare
You with the stars in your eyes
Making each day of the week
All my trials, Lord
No, nay, never

Do wah diddy diddy
Rocking, rolling, riding out along the bay
Everything is beautiful
And how you suffered for your sanity
Magic moments
Send in the clowns

John Matthias

WHILE REVIEWING JOHN BERRYMAN'S *THE FREEDOM OF THE POET*

By the time one gets into the middle and later essays, not to mention the several excellent short stories, there is some temptation to paste together a do-it-yourself Dream Song ...

Friends, the hovering and plunging grief
Exceptionally sings. Wow! We put
Against it, then, a pretty
Round-faced wench, who, with Alfred Kazin
And his wife, edited
Her fiction – ah! I thought –

And missed the boat. God amuses himself;
Then man. Both these facts have been forgotten.
Windmills grind wheat
From which, Sir Bones, our bread is made.
Irony To the end. Fair enough!
You may wonder whether I dislike aestheticians.

A high and prolonged riskiness?
The later Men just drudged along: Lowell into spondees
And humped smash. Hardy's
Reputation has been furiously unstable.
Tell you a story. Until
A writer begins to bore us, O, it is[1]

[1] *... a matter of supreme importance that he handle characteristic materials characteristically.*

Paul Muldoon

April in New Hope

Ascribe it though we may to the McCormick clan
The technology of the mechanical reaper and hay tedder
Had been developed by the Celts
Only to be lost with Rome. A Cambridge man
Might be done for by a 'bedder'
But Princeton men kept slaves. In 1849, the Corn Belt

Still stretched to the Delaware.
We few, we happy few, are still so newfangled
With our own Henriad
We forget New Hope is where
Each generation is doomed to wrangle
The shad roe from the shad

Only to pair them once again, fried in bacon fat
And served on a white platter
With capers and lime.
By 1949, Richard Feynman was already plugging away at
The idea of antimatter being matter
That merely goes backwards in time.

Eiléan Ní Chuilleanáin

The Signorelli Moment

She's back. Key in the door,
Dr Proteus feels giddy. Was this the house?
Didn't she remember
a frescoed wall with resurrected limbs?
There's a thump of a hoover, a radio plays,
a dead person greets her.

She's dead too, she thinks. A smooth nude
salutes a skeleton and gestures to introduce
while another levers
a strong thigh-bone out of white clinging clay.
Flesh has fallen away.
Politeness covers,

Dr Proteus considers. She looks around
for the service entrance, and finds
backyard, rubbish bins,
a fire-escape. She climbs, inhales,
but something grips her by the ankle,
means business.

Julie O'Callaghan

OUR HOUSE

I'm in it right now
maybe the satellite of you
can detect
the sonic boom
of me
wailing?

I'm transmitting
emergency radio waves
to whatever dark matter
you are now
sailing along
in your ship of death.

I had a house in Ireland
I had a life
I had a grocery list.
Do you see me?
Star I'm gazing at:
blink once for yes.

Michael O'Dea

Honora likes Hughie.
When Hubby's out, Hughie's in;
when Hughie's in, Hubby's out.
With pencil and jotter he arrives,
collaboraciously inclined towards writing poetry;
Honora fucks him poetic.

And he humping with winsome wordplay,
peppering words indiscriminate,
till catching the ribbon
pencilling at speed,
jostling his poultry,
he fillets his jotter with creation,

his wordels – love children.
Humpy happy
Hughie lozenges back on the pillow,
his foot writing,
receding tides have always been creative
on the sands.

Nessa O'Mahony

'AND THE SOUL CREEPS OUT OF THE TREE...'

for Louise Glück and John Berryman

the way out, a c-section of exposed bark
where the feller swung his axe
too wildly for neatness.
Now here and there
along the lake's reed shore
stumps like so many molars

left behind by a dentist high
on his own laughing gas,
no trace of the famed view
that launched a thousand haikus.
The wind lifts;
the balcony door shifts

wide enough to ask us
if red still matters,
regardless of function.
Two desks, two chairs;
one writes, one taps sweet
nothings: nothing sweet here.

Leeanne Quinn

EMERGENCIES

After a two-hour wait in a brightly lit room
you return to me and it's true to say
we leave here in better shape
than we arrived – the bus journey, a sway
of bodies in the unexpected sun.
The smell of hops coming in off the river

like something human on the air.
And though you swear you don't remember,
you were right, the passengers did stare,
the man who spoke beneath his breath
said what you thought he said – *dreams*
have their own geographies –

Yes, everything happened
just as you perceived, strange how we sense
impending casualty, stranger still
how the ambulance sped by, its siren signalling
a soul's misfortune, wailing blindly
in the wrong direction.

David Rigsbee

APPROACH

Off the starboard wing a light;
another plane winked by far below,
light pulsing in the step and steep
of Blake: *weep weep, weep weep*.
Arrows indicated how to deplane
from the wing. That was the word –

'deplane,' – but not the thought
of the word any more than 'thot'
spelled what our minds did
in the dim fuzzy distance where
lightning flared once, a newly lit
lantern (again, where?), and into turbulence

we went, the stiff wing flapping
like an angry heron (my line of sight went
straight out to the moon) startled
by some sly, brutal faces, intruding when
we scrutinized trusted mirages below: stars,
pockets, embers, archipelagoes.

Jane Robinson

After 10

For this performance she lies on bare bedsprings,
mortal with the *thinky death.*
Henry's gagged and bound in orange string.
Sailed a boat whose wood had rotted,
snapped mast wrapped in stays, rudder stowed
under a henhouse. They peck

and worry old boxes of paper.
She's plaintive, restless, the doctor
left long ago. Imaginary bones being no
replacement. And the others afraid of the jackdaw
(coat thrown
over the cage, cunt-pull of her finger-fed beak)

they left too. Like riding a bike,
you don't forget. She's sunk, so hopeless
she might try again, sort through those stones
one more time. *Is there anybody out there?*
Friend's missing – stage right, no one – nowhere.
Progressive deterioration, he liked.

John Saunders

SHELLS

As you shuffle towards me
I am reminded of you reaching
into coops to remove
freshly laid eggs heavy with fullness.
You are closer to that shed of forty years ago
than to me now.

In the corridor, your deafness a barrier,
you demand to leave –
to cross the road
to Murphy's, on the corner –
near the graveyard,
your history in front of you.

Nearly a century on from your birth
you bring the nest of the past
to protect your empty shells,
your solitary day interrupted
by an anonymous face,
you, searching a jaw bone for familiarity.

Gerard Smyth

GLIMMERINGS

(A Minnesota Dream Song)

The first day in Minnesota is always the worst.
Your body-clock lives in two places at once,
you only want to sleep but outside it's vintage America,
the school bus waiting for latecomers,
the garbage collectors raising dust.
High-steppers practise their twirls
on the stadium grass.

The way the weather breathes into your ear
is like a snake's hiss.
The pilgrim settles into the bunkhouse –
a room paid for in advance.
He has come a long way
to where his mission is to find those *glimmerings* again –
among the tree-shapes, along the ridges
or down the track to a panoramic vista
that seems to whisper lines from Whitman:

Night on the prairies,
The supper is over, the fire on the ground burns low.

George Szirtes

We do not dream, we arrive. Here
at the station, the waiting room. And nothing
arrives is the gloom of it.
It is Saturday and maybe summer. The silence
is weekend loud. Once there were wolves
in the empty cupboard. Gone.

And something touched my face, possibly
a sheet of newspaper or a bird's wing, or
the latest thing in transit
which is this, dare I call it. It was altruism
by any other name. It was the real thing.
It was Saturday and dying.

You hears me I guess. We hear in some fashion
of hearing. And the face, maybe no more,
and no bird or paper
or a train just arriving like a sudden noise
in the head. But one, waits, is waiting
for a wolf to bay and wait.

David Wheatley

Beard Song

Chinny chin chin, I spared you those years,
wrapping you tight in the seaweed tangle
of my first beard. In the confraternity
of the hirsute did I seek cover,
absorbing my frothings as I went,
and fed my beard on stout foam and slops.

There is a photo of the young Longley
and Mahon with the wrong one wearing the beard.
The emperor Julian wrote a satire on beard-
haters, the *Mispogon*. May I beard you
in your lair, Parnell asked Kitty O'Shea.
Poor cowering I, wearing my beard as a beard.

O beard, up you would look now and ask me,
Who's there, who *are* you? Baring my chin's
bum-cheeks to the wind, down what plug-hole,
I wonder, did you depart. I try on the face
I used to wear and, What is this, the ghost
of my beard bristles, some kind of ventriloquist act?

1990s

Nerys Williams

Refrain

(for Dream Song 14)

Perhaps it is always flamboyance
that flies in the face of the commonplace.
See this – winks the hand
to the skein of an eye –
These were once stars
on a commandant's shoulder.

And what? It can always begin again
in the poem that fits the furlong.
Winding and binding
in this intestinal wait
for something to happen.

It could always be found
in the accommodation of here and there.
As light streams against
the mahogany leaf, finding its
form in the gesture of
a signing bird in the eaves.

Macdara Woods

Nor would Signorelli do a Perugino rolling eye
As darkly, sometimes, Jacob did, alone,
Orbs ascending in fierce frenzy, neither love nor ether
Could assuage: he walking bareassed
Up the stairs, come small hour, two a.m. Old burns
Upon the knees and elbows. Of his skin.

After, O too many, years to come to this, unstable
Naked exile. Jacob knows, that transience is all,
& all is vanity, & that standing still
And moving on are much the same:
And matter less. Depends,
At base, on where you're looking from.

The monster in the morgue had monstrous rings
Made from glass eyes of the dead. Finer
To fondle wounds & larval mouths & eyes: & after death
The blow-fly, truth. Ovid, could read,
With the soles of his feet: O, well enough,
At least, to keep the traction taut.

Homage to John Berryman,
reading on stage in London, 1967.
All Henry, unforgettable.

Part II

Robert Archambeau

WE MUST NOT SAY SO

Sadness was he ever. Teacher, taught
my teacher, taught me too (his being not
in body but in book). 'What is the boy now
who has lost his ball?' he'd ask. The question's flawed.
'What, what' he'd ask 'is he to do?' A haughty Henry'd
huff his loss, a stone his daily broken bread.
And yours and mine? Is what he wrought?
Sadness we are ever, teacher taught.

'No use,' he'd say, to say 'O there
are other balls,' the ball gone harbor-wise,
and out, the tidal-tugging way.
No use to whistle 'I am not a little boy.'
For him a hurting. Us, maybe a sigh.
No laws against our Henry but 'Beware.'

Anthony Caleshu

I AM HENRY AGAIN

I am Henry again and because I am Henry
the police and the doctors and the teachers and these
old friends who are not so old nor so friendly are asking:
why this ice cream all around us? Why these libraries
and hospitals? Why these children and their dogs? The last
time I listened to anybody was as a child and I was
disappointed with the results. But just whose results were
they?
I forgot to ask as I licked the pink from my lips.
My resolve to know why the pink flowers
that glow in the moonlight smell like the woman I love
is unresolvable. I am and she is living again
with the animals under the stairs, for whom we care
with duty and just the right amount of neglect.
We are the reason people get born again
into mansions, living lives where manners are written
slowly,
word by word, until their meanings unfold like a
tablecloth.
And it is not musty. No, no. At dinner tonight,
our faces will glow with spumoni and spoons
long after the *maître d'*, like a magician, pulls the cloth
away,
taking with it the table.

Moya Cannon

THE HANG-GLIDERS

for Jean O Donnell and Nico Bernier

This afternoon we saw them,
huge rainbow-coloured butterflies,
high above us as we swam in the lake –
so many of the sons of Daedalus
who, in search of that ever-longed-for lightness,
run and jump off a cliff,
steer themselves about for hours in the air
skim mountain ridges,
levitate on thermals
and, almost always,
avoid assumption into storm clouds.

Later we pass them,
two-legged, tanned mortals,
in shorts and t-shirts, who solemnly
lay out their sails in the shade.
They fold and pack with exquisite care,
each cord, each of the pleats
on which their lives depend, in order.

And in the botanic gardens,
the huge butterflies emerge
from their upside-down capsules,
first the head, the strong front legs,
pressing against a papery cockpit lid,
and then, tumbling out slowly,
those exquisitely crumpled wings.

Harry Clifton

FROM *THROAT SONGS*

Wrecker's Lantern

Uncharted, brightening,
Fading, vanishing into black –
The wrecker's lamp. Or is it a lighthouse
Sending out its brilliant track
Of signal or semaphore
Across the muffled snore

Of waves in the night,
Of a chest gone tight?
If Christ could walk on water
Sleep is the glass-bottomed boat
I make my bed on.
Lying weightless, self afloat

On darker self –
The blue on blue, going down
Through lung-tree, peristaltic valve,
Breathing, making itself known
From beyond the continental shelf
And the realm of the drowned.

'A light that never was
On land or sea...'
I see it, and it frightens me,
Dilating, between three and four –
Sternum-wreckage, legend, loss –
On the other shore.

Michael Coady

BENEDICTION ON THE SIXTEENTH DAY OF MAY

Blessèd be his bad heart which allows him leave
to rest in sunshine on a broken chair
on this feast day of Brendan, voyager.
Close by his wife is on her knees
attending to her planting,
her strawberries and aubergines
her broccoli and beans and weeds
here in the former convent grounds
beside the river,

and blessèd be that river,
sister river of three sisters
its weirsong and its ancient bridge,
and blessèd too be Clareen Well behind him,
the fire station and the main road to Clonmel,
to all points west and back, with all its human
traffic and its transience.

Birds on every side sound out their manifestos
yea, even rooks and jackdaws rasping out
staccato climax of their *sacre du printemps*.
We're part of some great symphony
he thinks to tell his wife, but leaves
the obvious unsaid since they both seem
so tuned and yet so different
within this place and time.
Blessèd be not saying
when there's no need to say.

These days, he begins to feel
the weight of all the times
he's been around the star that fuels
all this, begins to wonder at how life

and time have taught him
less and less of certainty –
though in some deeper way.
He recalls his mother musing towards the end
Do I remember this or did I dream it?

What matter either way?
The winter past was one of storming
nights and days that brought their share
of last processions touching on their lives –
neighbour, friend, acquaintance
followed by the walking living,
heads bent against the weather
as they crossed the bridge, the river,
to the bone-yard on the hill.
Blessèd be the bone-yard
and the bent heads that live on.

He looks up to the east;
the town clock tower above West Gate,
the sun-warmed salmon and the bell
that soon will strike four on this afternoon.
Hear a key change in the river as the current slows
signalling a shift of earth and moon and sun:
another tide surprises, slipping in,
taking its time to probe, lay siege
and rise until weirsong
for now is overcome.

Blessèd be the broken
chair he rests upon.
Blessèd be the woman
kneeling on the earth.
Blessèd be the stillness
as the river holds its breath.

Theo Dorgan

What Wonders

Oh Mr. Bones I tell you it is hell,
to love, and love well, and be not desired.

But Henry, Henry, at our age love is grim,
moment by moment face to face with death,
facing eternity in the here and now,
waking in panic not to hear her breath.
We love, and lie there as the light grows dim
holding the well-loved other back from death.
What would I, waking, breathing here and now
not give, the half of what once I would get
for blood as hot as yours? You have it yet,
the pulse of life that I now half forget.
Desire? The body kindling to time's glow?
Henry! This life we have is touch and go.

Dave Lordan

When I was a monk

for Máighréad Medbh

When I was a monk or whatever it is that I was
for a breeze in the big wooded days out the west
there was only one book which I portioned aloud
to myself on a Sunday, cud-chewed the rest of the week.

For art and characters I lay on the moss-swaddled slab
of a thousand year Chief, watched shape-changing shapes
ceaselessly drift without plot, then dissolve in a sun
wheeling round to a moon that put me into a trance.

I saw thunderous battles in the epicing stars.
There were no repeats. I was never bored. Weather
was my living music – unscorable, mercurial, diverse;
varying season's of trees, birds, animals, grasses, insects,
seas –

mutable wind's modulations of these; innumerable rains
on the tracks, on the lake, down on hives, down on huts,
down on limestone, on granite, canopies, thatch...
Occasional monsoonish burstings that freshened the airs

and galvanised armies of ants.The river whose noises
were never the same. My own organic back catalogue.
Sometimes, passing by near a cliff or a bank a man on
a skiff would be singing of his mother's death to his
daughter.

Or she'd be laughingly singing of newborns to him.
That would do me for a year. I heard angels in sessiles
and demons in yew stands disputing my soul. What harm?
All who have souls are disputed and split. Soldierly

drumming from slopes near the fjord; from which
slope exactly, who knew? I couldn't care less.
No-one can steal from a man who has nothing to give
only brotherly silence in the fathomless silence of God.

Each spring I would stroll a few days to the coast,
and heave out as deep and as cold as I could
– waking my bones and my joints for the Summer.
With good-natured porpoises I glided and dove,

gargling along in their gargletalk as if I were one
of their brood. Each August I stood in a meadow
of storms, my palms stretched up rod-height.
I was struck once or twice by magnificent lightning

from Gabriel's sword. My brain bloomed like a desert
bush. I was nothing but fire in those instants.
One day I fished a blue baby girl from the lake.
I shrouded her in my own black rags. In the flittering

shades of an ash grove on the bank, ululating wildly
to frighten off animals, I scooped out a grave
and I buried her, with all available ceremony.
For 25 years I did kneel there and weep there

whenever I happened to pass. Daily, I noticed new curls
to a bird cry, new insects I refused to pin through with a name.
Names are a hex on God's bounty. Extinction begins with a
name.
Above all I saw – but it was more than a seeing –

how the world stays unowned and unmarked in its
infinite business like an infinite song only sung by itself
inside its own hearing. No matter who for five minutes
yaks in his vanishing tongue of squaring a rood

in the flow of this world, driving stakes through fire and flood.

Thomas McCarthy

Berryman in a Storm of 2014

A storm empties its garbage along Jackson.
Midsummer leaps from the Liquor Store
In a tantrum of rain – Mr. Bones, it ain't
That you you you wish to disremember
What Minnesota does in discreet darkness;
I can't recall the compact and delicious young
But the name of that one, that one, and that one,
A true name belonging to one Mr. Berryman,
Mr. Berryman drenched with hail
And thinkin' darkly on a high bridge
Between Sweden and St. Paul. Nobody falls.
But the names rise like steam from the grill
Of a Mississippi in spate; friends, Sir Bones,
Like that Navigator who played for Portugal,
That man ever remembered in Vietnam,
That maker of Ford, that (Mr. Bones) hapless
Kidnapper of the heiress Mary Pike.
The embankment buzzes. I advance upon
The hope of a name. In history as on Mars
All tyrants will seem to float below;
You and the husband, and the nameless
Others, stand on these Guthrie steps.
We watch it all go wrong in the river below.

Hugh Maxton

TOTE STADT

i.m. Peter Doherty. Born Llandudno, 1943. Died Budapest, 2009

1.

Came to sort it out, majestic shaded,
In digestic rum hotel
Where Bones stayed through bouts of writing
With John of Tyrone, ditto of Jordan.
In some low attic, soused a poem
Or fifty, doing pretty high things
By free fall, delicacy as brutal
Self-knowledge, fecked not made.

The unrecognised retreat on Henry
At mine silver or sliver monitor,
Shifty-shifty, the fault not theirs.
Photo here, a pee-dee-eff unspelled,
Measured fate-of-the-art footfalls
Sit tight. Who am the one and only peers
In the frames of subject? Gazes soar
For a keener flummery.

At the New Ga-ghallery opening
A journalist is beaten in the jacks
For thinking out of turn. Timeless the word
And deed, construction and ample art
Filtering into history like blood and piss
Together, the beaters undeterred.
Upstairs the elect and invited relax,
Muck a last picture show of the living.

Beckett is off the banned list though he used
The word spoken by none. Our troubles

Now are ended, watch the lad in thigh-long
Boots straddle yur one's shadow with pleasure.
Noises off, rough stuff on the cutting floor,
Deviced martyr lashed to a pylon.
From deep water, graveolent bubbles
Gravitate backwards to the much amused.

2.

Doherty appealed to few scouts, Welsh-born
By accident, Hungarian dying, a brilliant
Old phraser fashioned up to the minute.
He looks away in the picture, bluntly shy,
The glass half full, the life half less empty,
Exile English spoken with definite
Openness of heart, and curses pliant-
Ly generous, sweet thorns in plenty's horn.

Once begun, the thesis on Rosenberg
Was shotten down midchapter, riddled
With possibilities like and unlike Isaac.
The Book of Doherty stayed unwritten
Till he died of work, love, talk and inspiration,
His last words penned, pendulous with lilac-
Bloom of a railway-shaken neighbourhood,
Thrown rare coins uncashed for an exergue.

His dust came home to rest between Parnell
And numberless dumps of betrayed infants
In the national charnel house, Crass Nephin,
A trudge from Hopkins the Church destroyed
For Paddy Dignam's pence.
'Ireland sober
Shall never be at peace,' Doherty warned heaven
The last day we met,
and curtsied banks,
Belly-worship, *aperatifs* of Hell.

3.

Don't ask me to tie things up in the last
Analysis with a celebration
Of my friend's achievements home and away.
The gallery is for rogues, remember?
And today's rogues disinherit the earth.
Enough to allow him a refuge
From fat money's relentless abrasion
Of the heart, the dream, even the rest.

Someone, of course, had said it all before,
With shagged panache – 'The secret is not praise',
Invoking Mr Bones on occasion,
Prepared to receive Doherty
Among images of nearly evening,
Dusk in his non-native funereal town.
All ours to bear, with mohair-coddled lice
Fouler by thirty years and more future.

Paula Meehan

FROM *GEOMANTIC*

THE MEMORY STICK

I searched high, low, all over the place
growing more anxious by the minute:
a whole summer's work in a square inch
cohesion of metal and plastic –
an ode, an elegy, a ballad,
a sonnet flawed by its rhetoric
but still retrievable at a pinch
if I could recall where I put it,
the memory stick in its shiny case.

THE FLOOD

It was only when it receded
we knew it for the gift it had been.
If truth be told we missed the water.

It was exactly what we'd needed.
We missed the way it made a mirror –
doubled goose, godwit, egret, heron;

and that once in moonlight we looked down
on two complete and drowning strangers,
those depths where later wolfbane seeded.

John Montague

Happy Hour

A note to celebrate our days together,
Memories to warm that dank Dublin winter,
Hot toddies in Beggars Bush as you distil
Another run from your fermenting Dream Songs.
I was still young, aghast at genius,
Concerned with your comfort, a practical worshipper.

Later you came looking for me in Paris.
Claude Esteban found you on his doorstep;
White-bearded, demanding in stentorian tones
'Où est le poète irlandais?' and
Claude soft-footed across the way:
'Il-y-a un Moïse américain que te demande!'
Behind him, Henry Pussycat, grinning from ear to ear.

Gerry Murphy

You Did and You Did

A blank page in eternity
to you Berryman
and Dante and Virgil
to greet you on the other side.
An honoured place
in the First Circle
and the fee waved graciously aside
by the ferryman.

Tim Nolan

St. Mary's

For John Berryman

The hospital I was born in –
you walked away from.

I was carried out by my father.
You were carried all your life

by that grief made by your father
that morning near the back stoop.

St. Mary's was where Catholics
were born and died and dried out

if they found themselves in Minneapolis.
At the AA meetings – you must have been

moved by that vibration – call him
God – call him *Lord* – that coincidence

of insight from experienced
mechanics with a few good words.

It was inevitable – *the vibration* –
would take a literary turn –

that you would come back
to that urge for eloquence

within the marks and signs
of a weary but snappy line.

I too have no idea whether
we live again. I too *believe*

that I sit in this green chair –
which seems to be enough for now.

I always listen closely to your prayers –
before I get up to go –

Michael O'Loughlin

The Literary Life

In my room on the top floor
There are no blankets, so I sleep,
Like a Russian poet,
Beneath my sheepskin coat.
As in a child's angry fantasy, I eat
What I like for every meal: bread and cheese
And cold beer from exotic bottles.
On the table, the only other furniture,
Is my typewriter, an *Erika* made in the DDR
And biographies of Berryman and Lowell
Which I am reading in stereo,
Once again taking a cautionary tale
For a user's manual (I made
the same mistake with Joyce and Ellman).
I'm trying to write a poem about them,
Going for a kind of jaunty doggerel:
'*You poor old sods*
You thought you were gods
Or the nearest thing to it:
Greatest Living American Poet...'
The final lines will have something to do
With the 'Your move, Cal' note anecdote.
It's not working. Down four flights
Of coffin-defying stairs
The streets of Amsterdam are full of muses
But I need to sleep. I lie down
And watch from my bed
The solemnly, blackly dust-jacketed Haffenden
With its iconic portrait (maybe in McDaid's?)
And the fatter, yellow- covered Hamilton
(American edition), with its thick luxurious paper,
A gas-guzzling Cadillac of a book.
All this, I think, will someday

Be like that, as I fall asleep
Eyeing the tomb-like volumes,
Carefully trying to avoid seeing
The few scattered sheets of paper
The white overwhelming
The tentative ants' column
Which tomorrow will march on
When, unlike Berryman,
I will wake regenerate.

RICHARD RYAN

BRIGHT SAILS

(On the death of John Berryman, 7 January, 1972)

I

Blind harper, blind
fiddler, blind poet;
old hold-alls stuffed

with rags and ragged
dreams, petty session
held in ditch and shebeen.

The wise threw bright sails
to the wind and dropped
dead in their dreams

between candle and quill,
rats busy at them in
Hamburg cellar, Paris slum.

II

And now, again the old story.
Lamps guttering, over dark horizons
they lurch once more,

all our confused galleons
staggering in tempest,
collapsing under the weight

of their priceless cargoes.
On the rocks they flounder
toward, the girls glitter and sing

the gifts of their bodies
opening like wounds, as once again
on a far horizon the dawn sails by

like a world that works,
brown men singing in its rigging,
a golden fleet forever sailing the wrong way.

8 January, 1972

Peter Sirr

ROAD SONG

This is it
the cart-track, butter-path
the rumoured *tóchar*
unmissable, narrowest
of narrow causeways
along which, again,
the vagrant heart
sets out

stone heart dirt-flecked
sand-rained, berried,
snagged, feasting
and famished, loping
from one end to another

I stand on a stile
inhaling field, inhaling sea
close the gate
where goats bleat
and old cars rust in the grass

boreen to mountain
dunegrass to sea
my geography of desire
the poem steps before me
crossing a stream
climbing the stony path

bramble heart, harried
and stumbled, lifted
and slowed, paused in the gap
nailed to itself

on its way to you.

Joyce Sutphen

Berryman's Hands

Watching him on *YouTube* as he recites
self-consciously, overdoing it,
'Life, friends, is boring' and then comments
on *Anna Karenina* and how he made
Henry, part tragedy, part disaster, with
some humor, but highly exaggerated,
I notice his white and slender hands, how
tapered and long his fingers are
as he smoothes his moustache and rubs
his beard, saying words as if by heart,
stealing a quick glance at the page
from behind his horned rimmed glasses.

Once I saw him leaving Walter Library,
cutting across the mall on his way to
give a lecture in Ford Hall. I should have
dropped everything and followed him
to hear about Stephen Crane – 'that great
poet' or Mistress Bradstreet or the Bard,
but he was talking wildly to himself,
pausing as if he heard another voice,
which he did (and I, that day, did not).

Vincent Woods

INDIANA DAY

for Henry and John

Praise the day, the luminous day
When car is bird and bird is free
To circle the hills of Bloomington
A yellow flash of winter sun

Praise the friends who carry light
Who kiss the hand, and turn the wheel
The gruff and graceful men who steer
The winnowed crop to harvest store

Praise the force that brought us here
In tattered masks, on stumbling way
That led us safe past asylum gate
Past flash of war and pits' dark call

Praise the poet who named the Good
The sacred stop in the pulse of time
Shadows fracture house and farm
A chrysalis stirs in abandoned stone

Enda Wyley

Dream Song

Three visitors
came to my house.
Three travellers weary
from what went before.

I didn't think a lot
about the journey,
the first one said,
until I was half-way there.

I didn't realise,
the second one sighed,
how much more
was possible.

It seems too late now,
the last one said.
And yet, all three agreed,
You have opened

your door to us,
the room is well lit,
the smell of food
rises from the table,

and from sleep
will surely come,
the privilege
of a new moment.

Maurice Riordan

Afterword: At the Orchid Pavilion

The undergraduate 'poets' of Cork in my day were well versed in Berryman. Our sozzled late-night discussions were enlivened with such locutions as 'he mutter spiffy' (any poet we admired), 'I figure, yup, you is bad powers' (whisky); and yes, since it was mostly a schoolboy-ish cadre, we were wont to launch into 'Love her he doesn't but the thought he puts / into that young woman...' My dog-eared copy of the *Selected* is dated May 1972: so a few months after his death on 7 January.

But I do not recollect reading the poems then in the light of the suicide. What drew me was the language. It was an eye-opener that poetry could be this noisy, offbeat, candid, so low-life, funny, and agile. I was a bit too unaware of the thin ice under the manic exhilaration and innocent, I suppose, of the earnest within the jesting:

> I am obliged to perform in complete darkness
> operations of great delicacy
> on my self.

A disciple of Yeats, Berryman wrote dry conventional poetry to begin with: 'complicated, nervous, and intelligent', according to Jarrell. He was a college professor and a diligent Shakespeare scholar. He could easily have been one of the forgotten academic poets of the mid century. The invention of 'Henry' changed that, liberating a dangerous and profligate energy. The songs are all over the shop – rants, and squibs, and daft obscurities. It's poetry as stand up, improvised riffs, with lots of learnéd mimicry and mischief. Even the all-purpose form, in 6-6-6 lines, points to the Number of the Beast. And what

Gematrian meaning is hidden in 77? There's an element of tomfoolery and performance, of Malachi Stilt-Jack, to it all.

And now, in retrospect, it seems Yeats may have been key to the mid-life reinvention. Berryman had absorbed the stuff about mask and anti-mask and he remakes it in a motley guise – in a low register, for one thing. But, like Yeats, he also recasts the materials of his life, the personal tragedies and those of his friends, to make up, in his case, a generational drama on a grand scale: 'I'm cross with God who wrecked this generation'. One of the best components of the Dream Songs is its elegies with their memorable pen-sketches, 'malice was a pimple down his good strong face' (Frost); 'Flagrant his young male beauty' ('Delmore, Delmore'). They add up to a general Fall, or some shared *hamartia* that results in a communal malaise where Henry sits in black despair: 'There sat down, once, a thing on Henry's heart / só heavy....' In terms of the Songs' internal drama, Henry's fate is sealed – as victim and scapegoat.

No doubt Henry's 'pelt' does 'much resemble' Berryman. They have parallel damaged histories. But everything is changed by the leap into self-dramatisation. Henry becomes the suffering author writ large and mock-tragic, full of plights and gripes. Guilt-ridden, infantile, ungrammatical, sexist, self-pitying, you could say he is the unreconstructed *id* let loose. As such, Huffy Henry is an anti-hero to the high-toned poet – an anti-Whitman, anti-Ginsberg, anti-'Cal' and Yeats, for that matter. To adapt a phrase from Kevin Young, he is bent not 'on success (the dream) but on failure (the song)'. His is a fractured tragi-comic ego: 'Mr Heartbreak, the New Man, / come to farm a crazy land.'

And then there's the interlocutor, the one who buttonholes Henry and provides the sweetest comic moments: 'there ought to be a law against Henry. – Mr Bones: there is.' Soon we sense he's always present, even when silent, an implied sardonic listener ready to make the timely intervention: 'Easy, easy, Mr Bones', when Henry veers dangerously self-destructive. The PC vigilantes have had some issues with this stereotype of the blackface minstrel (which Berryman took from vaudeville). But they miss his ancestry, that he is an internalised manservant and the voice of practical reason. He completes the age-old comic pairing: like Sancho Panza to Quixote, Jeeves to Bertie Wooster.

It's true Berryman's star waned in the 1980s and 1990s. In those drab decades, when we were all going to be better people, there was a reaction against the rampant – often fragile – male egos of the 1960s. Yet now, the great Dream Songs – surely some two score or so – blow green as before. They shake a flag at a world as broken as ever. Could any other poet from that era provoke such a gathering as the editor has assembled in this book? Or inspire such an eagerness to re-deploy, and with such resource and variety, the possibilities of language that Berryman opened up, and in the process establish his legacy in our own time?

For a poet who memorialised so vividly his own 'surpassing masters', who yearned for their approval and aspired to their celestial company, to have done so is to 'apply the greatest praise'.

ROBERT ARCHAMBEAU's books include *Laureates and Heretics: Six Careers in American Poetry* (University of Notre Dame Press, 2010), *The Poet Resigns: Poetry in a Difficult World* (University of Akron Press, 2013), and the poetry collections *Home and Variations* (Salt, 2004) and *Slight Return* (Argotist Ebooks, 2011). He is professor of English at Lake Forest College.

SIMON BARRACLOUGH is the author of the Forward-finalist debut, *Los Alamos Mon Amour* (Salt, 2008), *Bonjour Tetris* (Penned in the Margins, 2010) and *Neptune Blue* (Salt, 2011). He is the editor of *Psycho Poetica* (Sidekick Books, 2012) and co-author of *The Debris Field* (Sidekick Books, 2013). He is currently working on a new book and multi-media show entitled *Sunspots* to be published in 2015 by Penned in the Margins.

CIARAN BERRY's books are *The Sphere of Birds* and *The Dead Zoo,* both published by The Gallery Press. He directs the creative writing program at Trinity College in Hartford, Connecticut, where he lives with his wife and two sons.

STEVEN BLISS grew up in Sheffield, read English at Cambridge in the 1970s, and now lives near Oxford. He began to write poems six years ago: a few have been published. He has been reading John Berryman, with growing respect, for over 40 years.

MICHAEL DENNIS BROWNE is an emeritus professor at the University of Minnesota, where he taught for 39 years. A new collection of poems, *The Voices,* will be published by Carnegie Mellon University Press in 2015. He has written many texts for music, working principally with composer Stephen Paulus.

ANTHONY CALESHU is author of a novella, two books of poetry, and a critical study of the American poet James Tate. He is Professor of Poetry at Plymouth University in the southwest of England.

SIOBHAN CAMPBELL's books include *Cross Talk* (Seren, 2010) and *That Water Speaks in Tongues* (Templar, 2008) which won the Templar Poetry Award and was shortlisted for the Michael Marks Award. She is editor of *Courage and Strength: Poems and Stories by Combat Veterans* (Combat Stress, 2012). She is Associate Professor in English Literature and Creative Writing at Kingston University London.

MOYA CANNON's fourth collection of poetry, *Hands,* was published by Carcanet Press in 2011. Originally from Co. Donegal, she has spent most of her writing life in Galway. A winner of the Brendan Behan Award and the Lawrence O'Shaughnessy Award, she has edited *Poetry Ireland Review* and was 2011 Heimbold Professor of Irish Studies at Villanova University. She is a member of Aosdána.

WALTER CANNON is Professor of English at Central College in Pella, Iowa where he teaches courses in early modern literature and poetry. He co-edited *Who Hears in Shakespeare? Auditory Worlds on Stage and Screen* (Fairleigh Dickinson University Press, 2012). His chapbook *The Possible World* was published by Finishing Line Press.

HARRY CLIFTON is author of several collections of poems, most recently *The Winter Sleep of Captain Lemass* (Bloodaxe, 2012) and *The Holding Centre: Selected Poems 1974–2004* (Bloodaxe, 2013). His short fiction, *Berkeley's Telephone,* was published by Lilliput Press in 2000. *Secular Eden: Paris Notebooks, 1994–2004* (Wake Forest University Press, 2007) won the *Irish Times* Poetry Now Award. Ireland Professor of Poetry between 2010–13, he has also taught at universities in Bremen, Bordeaux, as well as in TCD and UCD.

MICHAEL COADY lives in Carrick-on-Suir, Co. Tipperary and is a member of Aosdána. A recipient of the Patrick Kavanagh and Lawrence O'Shaughnessy awards, his Gallery Press books are *Oven Lane and Other Poems* (1987), *All Souls* (1998), *One Another* (2003) and *Going By Water* (2009), integrating poetry, prose and photography. In 2005 he held the Heimbold Chair in Irish Studies at Villanova University, Pennsylvania and in 2008 a residency at the Centre Culturel Irlandais in Paris.

PHILIP COLEMAN is a lecturer in English Studies in Trinity College Dublin, where he specialises in American Literature and is Director of the M.Phil in Literatures of the Americas programme. He has co-edited *'After thirty Falls': New Essays on John Berryman* (2007) and is the author of *John Berryman's Public Vision: Relocating the 'scene of disorder'* (2014).

JONATHAN CREASY was born and raised in Los Angeles. He studied music at California Institute of the Arts under Charlie Haden and apprenticed with Peter Erskine and Jeff Hamilton. In 2007, he moved to Ireland and attended Trinity College Dublin, where he studied English literature. He is editor-in-chief at New Dublin Press and a contributor and reporter for RTÉ Radio 1. He is currently pursuing doctoral research on Black Mountain poetics and pedagogy in TCD.

TONY CURTIS was born in Dublin in 1955. An award-winning poet, Curtis has published nine collections. His recent collections are *Folk* (Arc, 2011) and *Pony* (Occasional Press, 2013). He has been awarded the Irish National Poetry Prize, and is a member of Aosdána.

GERALD DAWE has published eight poetry collections with The Gallery Press, most recently, *Selected Poems* (2012) and *Mickey Finn's Air* (2014). He has also published volumes of essays, including *Poets & Poetry* (2011) and (forthcoming) *The Stoic Man*. He is Professor of English and Fellow of Trinity College Dublin.

JOHN F. DEANE was born on Achill Island in 1943. In 1979 he founded Poetry Ireland and *The Poetry Ireland Review*. His awards include the O'Shaughnessy Award for Irish Poetry, the Marten Toonder Award for Literature, the Golden Key Award from Serbia, and the Laudomia Bonanni Prize from L'Aquila, Italy. A member of Aosdána, recent books include *Where No Storms Come* (Blackstaff, 2010), *Eye of the Hare* (Carcanet, 2011), and *Snow Falling on Chestnut Hill: New and Selected Poems* (Carcanet, 2012). His forthcoming collection is *Semibreve* (Carcanet, 2015).

PETER DENMAN recently retired from the Department of English in Maynooth University where he taught for many years. He is a former editor of *Poetry Ireland Review*. His most recent publication is a collection of epigrams, *Epigrammata*, from Astrolabe Press.

MAURICE DEVITT had a career in business before he completed the MA in Poetry Studies at Mater Dei, Dublin City University, with a thesis focusing on the poetry of James Wright, John Berryman, Charles Bernstein and others. He was recently shortlisted for a Cúirt New Writing Award, the Listowel Writers' Week Collection Competition and he was also selected to participate in the Cork Spring Poetry Festival.

ISOBEL DIXON grew up in South Africa, where her debut *Weather Eye* (Carapace, 2001) won the Sanlam and Olive Schreiner prizes. She co-wrote and performed in *The Debris Field*, a multi-media show about RMS *Titanic* (Sidekick Books, 2013) and is currently working with Scottish artist Douglas Robertson on a project linked to D.H. Lawrence's *Birds, Beasts & Flowers*. Mariscat will publish a pamphlet, *The Leonids*, in 2016, and her next collection will come out from Nine Arches in 2015.

TIMOTHY DONNELLY's most recent book, *The Cloud Corporation*, received the 2012 Kingsley Tufts Poetry Award. His chapbook *Hymn to Life* was published by Factory Hollow Press in 2014. A Guggenheim Fellow, he is a poetry editor at *Boston Review* and teaches in the Writing Program at Columbia University's School of the Arts.

THEO DORGAN is a poet, novelist, prose writer, editor, essayist and translator. He has written libretti and documentary film scripts, and is a broadcaster on radio and television. Among his recent publications are a libretto, *Jason and the Argonauts* (2004), the novel *Making Way* (New Island, 2013), the prose memoir *Time on the Ocean: A Voyage from Cape Horn to Cape Town* (New Island, 2010) and poetry, *Greek* (Dedalus, 2010). A new collection, *Nine Bright Shiners*, will be published by Dedalus Press in October 2014. He is a member of Aosdána.

TYLER FLYNN DORHOLT's most recent work is *Modern Camping,* which was selected for the Poetry Society of America's chapbook fellowship (PSA, 2014). He co-edits the journal *Tammy* and the film and writing journal *On the Escape*. He lives and teaches in Syracuse, New York.

MARTIN DYAR grew up in County Mayo. His debut collection *Maiden Names* (Arlen House, 2013) led to the award of a residency at the International Writing Program at the University of Iowa, and was shortlisted for the 2014 Pigott Poetry Prize and the Shine Strong Poetry Award. The recipient of two Arts Council bursary awards for literature, he won the Patrick Kavanagh Poetry Award in 2009.

ZACK FINCH is an Assistant Professor of English at Massachusetts College of Liberal Arts. He is the author of *Chiasmus,* a poetry and visual art collaboration with the painter Enrico Riley, and his writing has appeared in journals including *American Letters & Commentary, Boston Review, Caliban / Anglophonia, Denver Quarterly, ESQ: A Journal of the American Renaissance, Fence, Gulf Coast, Jacket2, Poetry, Tin House* and *The Wallace Stevens Journal.*

LEONTIA FLYNN has published three collections of poetry, most recently, *Profit and Loss* (Jonathan Cape, 2011), and a book about the poetry of Medbh McGuckian (Irish Academic Press, 2014). She has been awarded the Forward Prize for Best First Collection, the Rooney Prize, the Lawrence O'Shaughnessy Prize for Irish Literature and the AWB Vincent American Ireland Fund Literary Award for 2014.

MARK GRANIER's poems have appeared in various print and online magazines and journals, including *The New Statesman, The Poetry Review, The Daily Poem, Verse Daily* and *Poetry Ireland Review*. His poetry collections are *Airborne* (Salmon, 2001), *The Sky Road* (Salmon, 2007) and *Fade Street* (Salt, 2010). His new collection, *Haunt,* is forthcoming in 2015.

DAVE LORDAN was born in Derby, England, and grew up in Clonakilty in West Cork. In 2005 he won the Patrick Kavanagh

Award. His collections are *The Boy in The Ring* (Salmon, 2007), which won the Strong Award for best debut and was shortlisted for *The Irish Times* Poetry Now Award; and *Invitation to a Sacrifice* (Salmon, 2010). His *First Book of Frags*, a collection of short fiction, was published by Wurm Press in 2013. A new collection of poems is forthcoming in 2015.

THOMAS MCCARTHY was born in Co. Waterford in 1954. Having worked for many years in Cork City Library, he is now writing fulltime. His collections include *The First Convention* (Dolmen Press, 1978), and from Anvil, *The Sorrow Garden* (1981), *The Lost Province* (1998), *Merchant Prince* (1998) and *The Last Geraldine Officer* (2009). He has also published two novels and a collection of essays. He is a member of Aosdána and lives in Cork.

IGGY MCGOVERN is Fellow Emeritus in Physics at TCD. He has published two collections of poetry with Dedalus Press, *The King of Suburbia* (2005) and *Safe House* (2010). He edited the anthology *20|12: Twenty Irish Poets Respond to Science in Twelve Lines* (Dedalus/Quaternia Press 2012). His latest publication is *A Mystic Dream of 4* (Quaternia Press, 2013), a sonnet sequence based on the life of nineteenth-century mathematician, William Rowan Hamilton.

JOHN MATTHIAS taught for many years at the University of Notre Dame and is a Life Member of Clare Hall, Cambridge, where he was previously Visiting Fellow in Poetry. He has published some thirty books of poetry, translation, essays, and fiction. His most recent books are a three-volume *Collected Poems* (Shearsman Books) and the novel, *Different Kinds of Music* (Shearsman Books, 2014). He is Editor at Large for the *Notre Dame Review.*

HUGH MAXTON was present on the occasion of John Berryman's Dublin reading (John Montague chairing, John Jordan interrupting learnedly, Ronnie Drew refereeing fairly fairly). His first collection, *Stones*, was published in 1971; *The Noise of the Fields* (Dolmen Press, 1976) was a Poetry Book Society Choice. His first novel, *Twenty 16 Vision*, appeared in 2009 from Duras Press. A second, entitled *Happen*, is forthcoming. *Waking: an Irish Protestant Upbringing* (Lagan Press, 1997) is autobiographical.

PAULA MEEHAN was born in Dublin where she still lives. She was educated at TCD and in the MFA programme at Eastern Washington University in Washington State. She has published six original collections of poems, most recently *Painting Rain* (Carcanet, 2012). She has taught a workshop over the years, 'The Poem & the Dream' with Californian based dreamworker Juliet Clancy. She is a member of Aosdána and the 2013–2016 Ireland Professor of Poetry.

JOHN MONTAGUE's *New Collected Poems*, representing nearly six decades of work, was published by The Gallery Press in 2012. In 1998 he became the first Ireland Professor of Poetry, and in 2010 the French State honoured him as a Chevalier de la Légion d'Honneur. He has also published several books of fiction and non-fiction, most recently *The Pear is Ripe: A Memoir* (Liberties Press, 2007), which includes a detailed account of his encounters with John Berryman.

PAUL MULDOON's twelfth collection of poems, *One Thousand Things Worth Knowing*, will be published in January 2015.

GERRY MURPHY was born in Cork in 1952. His latest publications include *End of Part One* (Dedalus, 2006) and *My Flirtation with International Socialism* (Dedalus, 2010). A new collection is forthcoming in 2015 from Dedalus.

EILÉAN NÍ CHUILLEANÁIN was born in Cork in 1942. She is an Emeritus Fellow of TCD where she has taught since 1966. Her *Selected Poems* were published by The Gallery Press and Faber and Faber in 2008. Her latest book, *The Sun-Fish* (The Gallery Press, 2009) was shortlisted for the T.S. Eliot Prize and was awarded the Griffin International Prize for poetry in 2010. She is married to the poet Macdara Woods. She is one of the founders and co-editors of the poetry magazine *Cyphers*, and is a member of Aosdána.

TIM NOLAN was born in Minneapolis, graduated from the University of Minnesota with a BA in English, and from Columbia University in New York City with an MFA in writing.

He is an attorney in private practice in Minneapolis where he lives with his wife and their three children. His two collections, *The Sound of It* and *And Then* were published by New Rivers Press. His poem 'Red Wing Correctional Facility', is shortlisted for the 2015 Forward Poetry Prize.

JULIE O'CALLAGHAN has lived in Ireland since 1974. Her poetry collections include *Edible Anecdotes* (Dolmen, 1983) and *What's What* (Bloodaxe, 1991). Her collections, *No Can Do* (Bloodaxe, 2000) and *Tell Me This is Normal: New and Selected Poems* (Bloodaxe, 2008) were Poetry Book Society Recommendations. Her most recent poetry collection for children is *The Book of Whispers* (Faber and Faber, 2006). She is a member of Aosdána.

MICHAEL O'DEA is a teacher in Rathmines College, Dublin. Two collections of poetry, *Sunfire* (1997) and *Turn Your Head* (2003) were published by the Dedalus Press. A bilingual chapbook, *Felos aínda serra,* was published by Amastra-N-Gallar in Galicia in 2005, and in 2013 he co-edited *The Roscommon Anthology* with John O'Dea.

MICHAEL O'LOUGHLIN was born in Dublin in 1958 and studied at TCD. He is an essayist and translator as well as a poet, and has written screenplays for feature films. He has published five poetry collections, most recently *In this Life* (New Island, 2011). After decades spent living abroad, he now resides in Ireland again, where he has been Writer Fellow at Trinity, and Writer in Residence for Galway City and County.

NESSA O'MAHONY was born in Dublin and lives there. She has published three books of poetry: *Bar Talk* (iTaLiCs press, 1999), *Trapping a Ghost* (bluechrome, 2005) and *In Sight of Home* (Salmon, 2009). She teaches creative writing for the Open University and the Irish Writers' Centre. A fourth poetry collection, *Her Father's Daughter,* is published by Salmon in 2014.

LEEANNE QUINN was born in Drogheda. Her debut collection of poetry, *Before You,* was published by the Dedalus Press in 2012, a poem from which was highly commended in the Forward Prize for Poetry 2013. She lives in Dublin.

DAVID RIGSBEE is author of *School of the Americas* (2013) and *Not Alone in My Dancing: Essays and Reviews* (forthcoming, 2015), both from Black Lawrence Press. He is a recent recipient of a National Endowment for the Arts Fellowship in Literature and a Pushcart Prize. He is the author of critical studies of Carolyn Kizer (1990) and Joseph Brodsky (1999), whom he also translated, and has co-edited *Invited Guest: An Anthology of Twentieth Century Southern Poetry*, named a Noted Book for 2001 by the American Library Association.

MAURICE RIORDAN's *The Water Stealer* was published in 2013. His previous books include *The Holy Land*, which received the Michael Hartnett Award, *Floods* and *A Word from the Loki. The Finest Music*, an anthology of early Irish lyrics, is published by Faber in October 2014. Born in Lisgoold, Co. Cork, he lives in London and is editor of *The Poetry Review*.

JANE ROBINSON studied biology at TCD and the California Institute of Technology and lived for several years in the USA and in India before returning to Ireland. Her work has appeared in *Poetry Ireland Review, Poet's Bookshelf, The Stinging Fly, Southword, can-can, Poetry24, Science Meets Poetry, The Sunday Tribune, Census, Magma* and *Abridged*. She read at the Poetry Ireland Introductions Series in 2011 and won the Strokestown International Poetry Prize in 2014.

RICHARD RYAN is the author of *Ledges* (Poetry Ireland, 1970) and *Ravenswood* (Dolmen Press, 1973). After a period spent teaching literature in Ireland and the United States in the early 1970s, he led a distinguished career in the Irish diplomatic service which included postings in Dublin, Tokyo and London, and he served as Irish Ambassador to the Republic of Korea, the Netherlands, the Czech Republic and the Ukraine. In 2001 he was President of the United Nations Security Council. He retired in December 2011.

JOHN SAUNDERS' first collection *After the Accident* was published in 2010 by Lapwing. He is one of three featured poets in *Measuring: Dedalus New Writers* published by Dedalus Press in

2012. His second full collection, *Chance*, was published by New Binary Press in 2013. He was shortlisted in the 2012 Desmond O'Grady Poetry Competition and is a 2014 Pushcart Nominee.

PETER SIRR has published eight collections of poetry with The Gallery Press, the most recent of which is *The Thing Is* (2009), which was also the winner of the Michael Hartnett Award for 2011. *The Rooms*, a new collection, will be published by The Gallery Press in 2014. He is a member of Aosdána.

GERARD SMYTH was born in Dublin where he still lives. His seventh collection, *The Fullness of Time: New and Selected Poems* was published by the Dedalus Press in 2010 and appeared in an Italian translation in 2013. He was the 2012 recipient of the O'Shaughnessy Poetry Award from the University of St Thomas in Minnesota. He is co-editor of *If Ever You Go: A Map of Dublin in Poetry and Song* (Dedalus, 2014) which was Dublin's One City One Book in 2014. He is a member of Aosdána and Poetry Editor for *The Irish Times*.

JOYCE SUTPHEN grew up on a farm in Stearns County, Minnesota and teaches literature and creative writing at Gustavus Adolphus College in St. Peter, Minnesota. In March 2012, *House of Possibility*, a letterpress edition of poems, was published by Accordion Press, and her latest collection, *After Words*, was published in May 2013. She is the second Minnesota Poet Laureate, succeeding Robert Bly.

GEORGE SZIRTES has published some fifteen books of poetry and roughly the same number translated from Hungarian. His first, *The Slant Door* (Martin Secker and Warburg, 1979) was joint winner of the Faber Prize. In 2004 he won the T.S. Eliot Prize for *Reel* (Bloodaxe, 2004), and was shortlisted again for *The Burning of the Books* (Bloodaxe, 2009) and for *Bad Machine* (Bloodaxe, 2013). *In the Land of the Giants* won the CLPE Prize for best collection of poetry for children in 2013.

DAVID WHEATLEY was born in 1970 and lives in rural Aberdeenshire. He is the author of several collections of poetry with The Gallery Press, and the critical study *Contemporary British Poetry* (Palgrave).

NERYS WILLIAMS lectures in American Literature at UCD. She has published poems and critical essays widely and is the author of two monographs *Contemporary Poetry* (Edinburgh University Press, 2011) and *Reading Error: The Lyric and Contemporary American Poetry* (Peter Lang, 2007). Her first volume of poetry, *Sound Archive* (Seren, 2011), was shortlisted for the Felix Dennis (Forward) prize and won the Rupert and Eithne Strong First Volume Prize in 2012.

MACDARA WOODS was born in Dublin in 1942. He has published eighteen books, as well as recordings of collaborations with musicians, composers and graphic artists. A founder/editor of the literary magazine *Cyphers* since 1975, he has read his work from Buenos Aires to San Francisco to Moscow. His *Collected Poems* was published by Dedalus in 2012. He is a member of Aosdána.

VINCENT WOODS is a poet, playwright and broadcaster. He was born in Co Leitrim in 1960, lives in Dublin and is a member of Aosdána.

ENDA WYLEY's fifth collection, *Borrowed Space: New and Selected Poems* is published by Dedalus Press in 2014.